D1532088

ANGEL CATS

BY BONNIE ALTENHEIN

ILLUSTRATIONS BY MONICA SHEEHAN

WINGS BOOKS • NEW YORK • AVENEL, NEW JERSEY

This 1995 edition is published by Wings Books,
distributed by Random House Value Publishing, Inc.,
40 Engelhard Avenue, Avenel, New Jersey 07001,
by arrangement with the author.

Random House
New York • Toronto • London • Sydney • Auckland

Printed in Mexico

Library of Congress Cataloging-in-Publication Data

Altenhein, Bonnie.
Angel Cats / by Bonnie Altenhein; illustrations by Monica Sheehan.
p. cm.
ISBN 0-517-14669-X
1. Cats — Quotations, maxims, etc. 2. Cats — Caricatures and cartoons.
3. Angels — Quotations, maxims, etc. 4. Angels — Caricatures and cartoons.
5. American wit and humor, Pictorial.
I. Sheehan, Monica. II. Title
PN6084. C23A47 1995
818'. 5402 — dc20   95-24581
                                                     CIP

8 7 6 5 4 3 2 1

to angel cats everywhere,
and the people who love them,
especially Fluffy and Shana
and Mrs. Judi Mae Katz

— B.A.

to Michael, Margaret,
Kara, Jack and Meredith

— M.S.

Angel cats wear the brightest halos of all our feline friends. They always seem to know how you feel — nestled softly on your lap when you need a gentle hug, and never laughing at your baggy at-home sweats. Cats are non-judgmental, and love you love you just the weight you are. They share your good times and not so good times, your dish of ice cream, your love of re-runs and they always purr at your jokes.

So next time Fluffy or Bunky or Kitty-Poo plays catch with your designer glasses, or sweet little kitten rearranges all your socks, remember that kittens are a delightful way to start angel cats... and all cats are the angels' way of sending you love.

Cats are special angels
who love you just the
way you are.

Cats are special angels
who meow at your jokes
no matter how many times
you tell them.

Cats are special angels
who can see you
with their eyes closed.

Cats are special angels
who warm up
your side of the bed
on a chilly morning.

Cats are special angels
who help you with
the household chores.

A closed door is meant to be opened.

Cats are usually responsible for single-sock syndrome.

Cats are special angels
who can keep your
most precious secrets.

Don't cry over spilled milk.

Try to let sleeping dogs lie.

Cat angels love to go
on vacation with you.

Angel cats love to
watch re-runs
of "The Love Boat."

Cats are special angels
who share your love of culture.

Cats are special angels
who love how you
sing "Feelings."

Paw prints are an original decorating statement.

Angel cats are high-tech wizards with an amazing genius for your electronic toys.

Always shop from a *catalog*.

Assume this is your real life
and not the first of
nine chances.

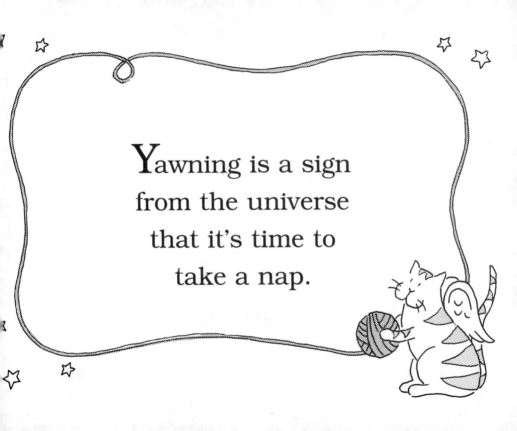

Yawning is a sign
from the universe
that it's time to
take a nap.

Nurture your inner kitty.

Cats are special angels
who share your dreams.

Cats are a sweet reminder
that love is nearby.

Cats are special angels
who are always interested
in your horoscope.

Don't pussyfoot around.

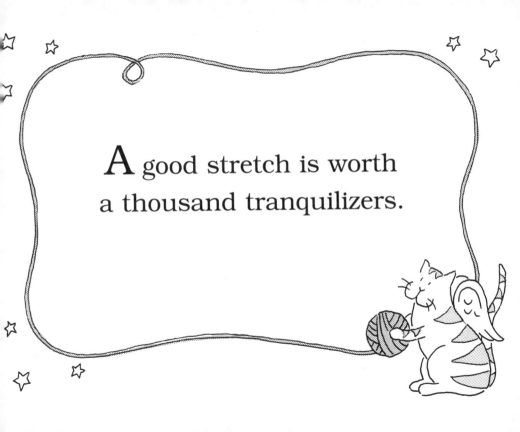

A good stretch is worth
a thousand tranquilizers.

Cats are special angels
who get sympathy pains
when you have the flu.

Cat angels listen
when you tell them
you had a terrible day.

Cats are special angels
who watch over you
while you sleep.

Anytime is the right time
for a catnap.

Take time to claw the furniture.

Refine your purr
until it is *purr*fect.

Angel cats appreciate your love
of the classics.

Cats are special angels
who can remember
the names of your
last four boyfriends.

Cats are special angels
who feel the way you do about
An Affair to Remember.

Just say "No" to catnip.

Practice being a switch swatter.

Sincere yawning and stretching
are aerobic exercise.

The world is your playground
and everything in it is your toy.

Cats are special angels
who love to exercise with you.

Cats are special angels
who are interested
in your career.

Cats are special angels
who bring you gifts
for no reason.

Cat angels understand
your creative fashion impulses.

Elevate adorable to
an art form.

Mystery loves company.

Cats are special angels
who give you your morning
wake-up call.

Cat angels save the last bit of milk for your morning coffee.

Cats are special angels
who know just where
you need a massage.

Cats are special angels
who love you in your
baggiest comfy sweaters.

Never trust people
without cat hair
on their clothes.

"Shalom," "Aloha," "Meow"
and "Purr" can mean
just about anything.

Cleanliness is next to godliness.

Cat angels can speak fluent Cat Latin and understand otherwise perfectly normal humans who sometimes forget English.

Angel cats give you
the remote control
some of the time.

Cats are special angels
who think a home-cooked meal
comes out of a can.

Practice having a whimsical meow.

It never hurts to ask
for what you want.

Cats are special angels
who love to play hide-and-seek,
find the socks and cat's cradle.

Cats are the first to volunteer
to help a good cause.

Cats are special angels
who think the crook of
your arm is their bed.

Cats are special angels
who are supportive of
your latest diet.

Inspire whimsy.

Angel cats voice their opinions.

Angel cats will love you
in the morning, tomorrow
and when you're 64.

Cats don't really wear pajamas.

Cats are the best teachers
of unconditional love.

Whoever said dogs are
a man's best friend
never had a cat.

BONNIE ALTENHEIN was born and raised in New York City, and has been writing about everything from angels to zebras since she was old enough to hold a crayon. She was editor of *Better Homes and Gardens* magazine, former secretary and "joke coordinator" for Joan Rivers, and creator of WATCH MY LIPS!—a unique, million-dollar company that developed a line of "greeting seed" cards that became an overnight industry phenomenon. She has been featured in *Business Week*, *Advertising Age*, and other publications.

Nominated several times for the "Louie" award—the highest honor for greeting card writers, Ms. Altenhein is a free-lance writer/designer and the author of a bestselling calendar, poster, and several greeting cards featuring angels. Her previous books are *How Angels Get Their Wings*, *Christmas Angels*, *Angel Love*, *Moms Are Angels*, and *Santa's Angels*.

MONICA SHEEHAN has illustrated numerous books, including *How Angels Get Their Wings*, *Christmas Angels*, *Angel Love*, *Moms Are Angels*, *Santa's Angels*, *The Toast Always Lands Jelly Side Down*, and *Quotations To Cheer You Up When The World Is Getting You Down*. She lives on the Jersey shore.